Shut Up and Listen

How to Save Your Relationship Using Active Listening Techniques to Increase Trust, Avoid Misunderstandings and Live a Happier Life with Your Loved One

Table of Contents

This example demonstrates a classic case of misunderstanding. Amy interpreted Bob's actions through her lens, and Bob was oblivious to Amy's expectations. Neither was wrong, but the lack of active listening and clear communication led to a rift in their relationship. When accumulated over time, misunderstandings like these erode the foundation of trust and mutual respect in a relationship.

Acknowledging and addressing misunderstandings with active listening is transformative. By actively seeking to understand your partner's perspective, you open the door to honest and empathetic communication. You will resolve conflict effectively and foster a sense of emotional safety where both partners feel comfortable expressing their thoughts and feelings.

The Essence of Active Listening

At its core, active listening is a journey to understand and connect with your partner. It only happens when you set aside your judgments and assumptions and immerse yourself in their world. Doing so demonstrates that you value and respect their thoughts and feelings, fostering emotional safety and trust.

Active listening is about more than just waiting for your turn to speak, and it is not offering solutions to problems. It's about being present at the moment, fully attuned to your partner's emotions, and providing them with space to be vulnerable and authentic without fear of judgment. In this deep presence, you listen to unspoken feelings and desires. Essentially, you are trying to understand what the words mean and what they mean to your partner. This empathetic connection lets you respond in ways that make your partner feel heard and understood, nurturing intimacy and an emotional connection.

The Benefits of Active Listening

By now, you're familiar with the concept and the fundamentals of this essential communication skill.

In this chapter, we delve deeper into the many benefits that active listening brings to your relationship. As we explore these benefits, you'll see how active listening can transform your relationships, increase your knowledge base, and enhance your overall well-being.

So, grab your notepad because we're about to uncover the remarkable advantages that await those who embrace the power of active listening. Let's dive in and discover how.

Start a Positive Communication Loop

When your partner feels genuinely heard and understood, they are more likely to listen to you. A conversation is a dance and not a battle—you are not waiting for your chance to speak but responding to your partner's words. Sometimes you will lead, and sometimes they will lead. Active listening fosters an upward spiral of emotional connection and understanding. When you really pay attention to what someone's saying, they feel happy and valued. You´re showing them that what they're saying matters to you. When you do this, something extraordinary happens. They want to know what you think too!

Imagine you're talking about something important to you, and your partner is really listening. They're not looking around or playing with their phone but focused on you. You'd feel awesome, right? And possibly, you become more willing to listen to your partner. When you make people feel awesome by listening, they also start caring about what you have to say. It's like a trick that makes both sides want to know each other's thoughts.

So, remember, when you take the time to hear someone out and understand what they're saying, they'll want to hear your thoughts too. It's like a magical way to make your bond even more robust. This is why you don´t have to read this book with your loved one, even if that is a great idea. Just by starting the communication by active listening, you will establish a positive communication loop.

Create Emotional Intimacy

Emotional intimacy comes through vulnerability when honest thoughts, feelings, and fears are shared. Active listening is the key to nurturing intimacy in a relationship. Being present and attentive creates a safe space for your partner to express their deepest emotions without fear of judgment or rejection. Through active listening, you validate your partner's feelings, showing them their emotions are acknowledged and respected. It fosters a solid emotional bond where both partners feel seen, heard, and understood profoundly.

Resolve Conflicts Effectively

Conflict is a natural part of any relationship, but how you handle it can make all the difference. Active listening is vital in conflict resolution, allowing both partners to express their grievances and concerns in a non-judgmental environment. Through active listening, you are not defensive to any verbal attacks and instead focus on understanding your partner's point of view, no matter how triggering it might be. The way your partner feels is valid, no matter what caused that feeling, and is more inclined to listen to you. Active listening de-escalates conflicts and finds common ground and mutually acceptable solutions.

Strengthen Trust

Active listening builds trust by demonstrating genuine interest and investment in your partner's well-being. When you actively listen, you show that you are dependable, which fosters security and trust in the relationship. By actively listening, you honor your partner's vulnerability, strengthening the trust and creating a solid foundation upon which the relationship thrives.

Nurture Emotional Support

Active listening is the foundation of emotional support—you can't support someone without knowing what help they need. By actively listening, you become attuned to your partner's needs, providing them with the comfort and reassurance they seek. This emotional support creates a sense of closeness and solidarity, making the relationship a safe haven for both partners. When you actively listen, you discover the root cause of problems and can provide support instead of taking issues at face value and trying to solve them.

Enhance Intimacy

Active listening creates a deep emotional connection. When you actively listen, you are more in tune with your partner's desires and needs, leading to a more fulfilling and satisfying physical and emotional intimacy. The emotional bond nurtured through active listening spills over into the physical realm, making the moments of intimacy more profound and meaningful.

Encourage Personal Growth

Active listening encourages personal growth and self-awareness. As you actively listen to your partner, you become more attuned to your emotions and reactions. A heightened self-awareness enables you to recognize patterns and triggers, leading to personal growth and self-improvement. Active listening leads to being open-minded and accepting of different perspectives, contributing to your overall development. Also, by listening to your loved one, you might get inspired, learn new things, and gain insight into areas you knew nothing or little about before listening.

Chapter 2: Empathy as a Foundation for Listening

Empathy is the special ingredient in active listening that deepens your connections with loved ones, adding a new layer of depth and meaning to your relationships. It involves stepping into their shoes and genuinely understanding and sharing their feelings without passing judgment. When you practice empathy, you temporarily set aside your own emotions and intentions, whether it's the desire to offer well-meaning advice or to relate **to** a similar personal experience. It's important to note that empathy doesn't necessarily mean agreement with your partner; instead, it signifies your willingness to stand with them, showing that you care and comprehend their perspective.

How do you do this? Your partner walks through the door after a tough day at work. You could respond with your usual quick fixes. Instead, you tap into your empathy superpower. You sense the exhaustion weighing them down, their frustration, and their longing for support. You're not just listening with your ears but feeling with your heart. And in that moment, you're there for them with genuine care and validation. You imagine what they must feel and try to understand how that affects them and how it would affect you.

In this example, John's wife, Sarah, comes home from work.

John: (looking concerned) *Sarah, I noticed you've seemed really stressed lately. Is everything okay?*

Sarah: (sighs) *Well, not really. Work has been so overwhelming, and I feel like I'm drowning in deadlines.*

John: (nodding and withholding his urge to tell Sarah about an app that helps prioritize work tasks he recently tried). *I'm sorry to hear that, babe. Tell me more about what's been going on.*

Sarah: (opens up) *It's just that my boss keeps piling on more work, and I'm struggling to keep up. Plus, I had that argument with my colleague today, and it left me feeling so frustrated.*

John: (listening attentively, choosing to ask Sarah to tell him more about the situation instead of judging her colleague) *I can imagine how frustrating that must be, especially when you're already swamped with work.* (pauses) *How did the argument start?*

Sarah: (explains) *We had different ideas about the project, which escalated into a heated argument. I hate confrontation, and it really shook me up.*

John: (compassionate tone, asking Sarah rather than suggesting a solution) *I'm sorry you had to go through that. It sounds like a tough day.* (pauses) *What can I do to support you?*

Sarah: (teary-eyed) *Just having you listen like this helps, John. It means a lot.*

John: (gently) *I'm here for you, Sarah, and I want to understand what you're going through. If there's anything else you want to talk about, just know that I'm all ears.*

In this dialogue, John demonstrates empathetic listening by showing genuine concern, asking open-ended questions, and offering support without judgment. His empathetic responses help Sarah feel heard and understood, strengthening their connection in their marriage.

Empathy turns ordinary conversations into extraordinary connections. It's a warm hug for your partner's emotions, showing them that you genuinely get them and that their feelings matter to you. So, next time you chat with your loved one, use your empathy superpower and stand shoulder-to-shoulder with your partner.

The Impact of Individual Experiences

Your life experiences are glasses through which you see the world. Your upbringing, culture, and the events that shape your journey all tint your lenses. This tint influences how you interpret situations, make snap judgments, and even form opinions. But here's the twist: your partner has a different pair of glasses with their unique tint too. This diversity of experiences sometimes creates a mix-up in communication and understanding.

Imagine two partners with entirely different notions about financial responsibility, all thanks to their upbringing. One partner grew up in a household where every penny was saved for the future, while the other comes from an environment where the value was placed on spending money to create memorable experiences.

Without a healthy dose of empathy, these differing viewpoints might become arguments, brewing conflict and lingering resentment. It's like trying to speak two different languages without a translator. Things just don't click! But that's where empathy steps in as the bridge that connects those two viewpoints, smoothing out the potential rough patches.

The Challenge of Being Non-Judgmental

Being non-judgmental is not always easy, as you are hard-wired to make quick judgments based on your personal experiences and beliefs. People often jump to conclusions or form opinions about others without truly understanding that person's experiences and motivations. In relationships, these judgments are detrimental to active listening. When you bring your prejudices and assumptions into conversations (slight or major), you shut down your partner's perspective, making them feel unheard and invalidated.

Being non-judgmental is essential to effective active listening. By setting aside your preconceived notions, you create a space where your partner is safe to share their thoughts and emotions openly. When you suspend judgment, you demonstrate genuine care and openness, fostering an environment of trust and vulnerability.

Being non-judgmental is one of the trickier skills to master. You must catch yourself in the act of forming an opinion before it clouds your judgment. Human brains have a knack for making lightning-fast decisions and judgments based on past experiences and beliefs. It's a valuable mental shortcut that sometimes leads us astray. In relationships, these snap judgments put up walls and hinder genuine active listening. They act like a roadblock on the path to understanding, making it difficult for your partner to express themselves freely. It's like trying to run with one foot stuck in cement-you're not going anywhere fast.

There's a silver lining. Being non-judgmental is another superpower that transforms your interactions. Picture yourself hitting the pause button on your assumptions and opinions, creating an open space where your partner's thoughts and feelings take center stage. You give them the green light to express themselves without being shut down or dismissed. And do you know what? When you do that, you're saying, "Hey, I'm here for you. I want to understand." This act of suspending judgment builds a cocoon of trust and vulnerability. Your partner feels safe to share their innermost thoughts, knowing you're genuinely interested and supportive.

The Practice of Non-Judgmental Listening

Non-judgmental listening is a workout for your empathy muscles. It's about being in tune with your biases and consciously putting them on the back burner when you engage in conversations. It takes a dash of self-awareness and a sprinkle of humility. You're basically saying, "Okay, I know I might have some preconceived notions, but I'm willing to push them aside for now."

And the fun part is that curiosity becomes your sidekick in this adventure. Instead of jumping to conclusions, you become a detective of emotions and thoughts. You ask questions like, "I wonder why they see it that way?" or "What could have led to this perspective?" It's like opening a treasure chest of understanding. You're not just hearing their words but exploring their motivations and feelings behind them. This curiosity is what helps you suspend judgment and keep assumptions at bay. It's easy to know what a conversation is about, but often challenging to understand what someone is communicating when you let the words get in the way.

Reflective listening is an amazing tool. You're having a chat with your partner about a recent disagreement. Instead of swooping in with your opinions or quick fixes, you hit the brakes. You pause and then say, "So, if I understand correctly, you're feeling frustrated because you think I didn't consider your viewpoint, right?" You put a mirror in front of them, reflecting back their thoughts and emotions. This technique creates a space for clarification and expansion. You give them a chance to say, "Yes, that's exactly it!" or "Well, not exactly, there's a bit more to it..." Reflective listening isn't just a communication hack; it's a magic wand that transforms conversations into meaningful exchanges.

The Transformative Power of Non-Judgmental

Listening

Imagine a world where conversations flow effortlessly, where partners feel safe to bare their souls, and where conflicts dissolve before they have a chance to escalate. This world exists, and its discovery lies in the transformative power of non-judgmental listening. It revolutionizes how you connect with your loved ones, paving the way for deeper understanding, emotional intimacy, and harmonious relationships.

One of the most remarkable aspects of non-judgmental listening is its ability to dismantle barriers and build bridges of trust. Think about a time when you felt truly heard and understood by someone. How did it make you feel? Chances are, it made you feel validated, respected, and valued. When you extend the same courtesy to your partner by practicing non-judgmental listening, you create a haven for them to share their thoughts, feelings, and experiences. This safety net encourages authenticity and vulnerability, laying the foundation for a deep emotional connection.

Non-judgmental listening acts as a lubricant for the gears of communication. Have you ever noticed how a conversation takes a nosedive when judgment enters? Partners become defensive or shut down, leaving issues unresolved and emotions simmering. When you choose non-judgmental listening, this open communication channel becomes a powerful tool for conflict resolution. Instead of trading blame or shutting each other out, you engage in a constructive dialogue where both parties feel heard and understood.

Non-judgmental listening is a catalyst for personal growth and self-awareness. Setting aside your judgments and immersing yourself in your partner's perspective opens the door to new insights and perspectives. This willingness to embrace differing viewpoints leads to a broader understanding of the world and yourself. You might discover hidden biases or assumptions you never knew existed, prompting a journey of self-discovery and growth.

Empathy is the foundation upon which active listening thrives. It allows you to step beyond your perspectives and truly understand and feel what your partner is going through. Being non-judgmental creates a space of trust and acceptance, enabling open and honest communication. Empathy and non-judgmental listening are essential guiding lights in the journey toward deeper connections with your loved ones. They illuminate the path to richer and more fulfilling relationships. So, embrace the power of empathy and strive to be a non-judgmental listener as you continue your exploration of active listening.

Chapter 3: Obstacles to Listening

Have you ever found yourself nodding along in a conversation while your mind races through a list of things to do or tried to remember the one connected thing you must add? Have you been caught in a mental loop of thoughts while your partner was sharing something important? Do you sometimes have the urge to give your loved one unwanted advice or tell them that they are actually wrong? The journey of active listening is challenging and transformative.

It's fascinating how a single mind can generate such an uproar of internal chatter, especially when trying to focus on someone else's words. This mental commotion often pulls you away from the present moment and blocks your listening, and when you can't listen, you can't hear. Whether it's the endless list of tasks at work, pondering dinner plans, or giving in to prejudices, these culprits cloud your listening space.

These pesky mental roadblocks divert your attention, cloud your understanding, and hinder the deeper connections you crave with your loved ones. So, roll up your sleeves and delve into the noisy world inside your head.

The Mental Hamster Wheel

You're engrossed in a heartfelt conversation with your partner, their words flowing like a gentle connection stream. You're nodding, maintaining eye contact, and genuinely trying to be present. Then, almost out of nowhere, your mind jumps onto a mental hamster wheel. Suddenly, the mental checklist of tasks that must be tackled before the day's end starts spinning furiously. Your thoughts have been hijacked, and you're now caught in a whirlwind of deadlines, appointments, and responsibilities.

Your partner's words become background noise as your mind races through its agenda. You might still nod and smile, but your focus has shifted, no longer on the conversation but on the mental hamster wheel that has taken center stage. You might even find yourself mentally rehearsing the steps of a task you need to complete or mentally rearranging your schedule to fit everything in. Meanwhile, the beautiful exchange has been interrupted, and the genuine connection you fostered is starting to wane.

This phenomenon isn't about neglecting your responsibilities or ignoring your to-do list. Instead, it's about recognizing that there is a time and place for everything when you're conversing with your partner that deserves your full attention. The mental hamster wheel, while relentless, can wait its turn. By allowing it to take over during a meaningful exchange, you unintentionally let it steal the opportunity for connection, understanding, and emotional intimacy.

The next time you find your mind wandering, try to take a deep breath and bring it back to the conversation before you, and if your mind has wandered extensively, don't be afraid to apologize and ask your partner to repeat themselves. It might frustrate them, but it shows you want to hear them.

Or maybe, your mental clutter or stress level is so high it deserves your attention before you can genuinely listen to your partner. Honesty is the key here. Tell your partner that you really want to listen but that too much is happening in your head right now. Ask for a moment to clear your head, write something down or send that important email. Then, come back to your partner with genuine interest.

Sneaky Prejudices

The intricate landscapes of thoughts and beliefs in your mind are fascinating and puzzling. Sometimes, they are the unexpected guests who arrive uninvited to the party of attentive listening. These guests take the form of hidden biases and preconceived notions. They also have a knack for quietly slipping into the conversation unnoticed. It's like inviting a friend over, only to realize they've brought along their opinions and judgments, subtly influencing the atmosphere.

These biases can be pretty crafty. They emerge as assumptions you make about others based on your past experiences, cultural influences, or societal stereotypes. It's as if your mind has a repertoire of scripts ready to be projected onto the stage of your interactions. For instance, you might unconsciously assume that certain behaviors are typical for a particular gender or quickly slot someone into a category based on their appearance. These scripts are like actors playing a role, shaping your perception, and influencing how you engage in conversations.

Consider this: your partner starts sharing her thoughts about an issue at work. She is describing a situation where she felt her contribution was overlooked. Suddenly, your mind's hidden biases chime in, whispering things like, "Typical women, it´s not a big deal, is it?" It's a shadow that sneaks into the conversation, casting doubt on the validity of her feelings. Or, you might catch yourself thinking, "I told her so. Women shouldn't work in that line of business." In an instant, your mind shifts focus from their words to your own prejudice, and you're no longer fully engaged in the exchange.

Recognizing and addressing these hidden biases is a crucial step toward effective and empathetic listening. It requires self-awareness to catch these biases and set them aside. You create space for authentic connection when you intentionally put these assumptions on the back burner. You allow yourself to see the person in front of you without the distortions of preconceived notions, and you invite their words to take center stage.

Distractions and Diverted Attention

In today's fast-paced world, distractions are everywhere, vying for your attention and tugging you away from the present moment. These distractions take various forms, from digital devices to wandering thoughts, and hinder your ability to be fully present and attentive.

The ping of notifications or the allure of social media can be irresistible. These digital distractions have a knack for stealing the spotlight from real-life conversations. Just as you're about to dive into a meaningful exchange, a quick glance at your phone can derail your focus. Before you know it, you're physically present but mentally miles away from the conversation.

Your mind is a skilled wanderer, often meandering through memories, worries, and fantasies. While your partner shares their thoughts, your mind might take an unscheduled detour to a completely unrelated mental landscape. This wandering steals your attention and leaves you grasping for the thread of the conversation.

The mind has an uncanny ability to dredge up past encounters, coloring your perceptions and anticipation of what's to come. As your partner shares a story, your mind might innocently chime in with, "Oh no, here it comes – she's going to talk about her colleague again." This preemptive assumption creates a mental barrier that hinders your ability to engage in the conversation.

And then there are those fleeting thoughts that tempt you to switch roles from listener to speaker. As your partner speaks, your mind starts constructing its response. It's a dance where you're constantly thinking about your next move instead of savoring the rhythm of the moment. These self-centered thoughts pull you away from the connection you're trying to build and place the focus squarely on yourself.

Amid these distractions, active listening becomes a delicate balancing act. It's about recognizing when your attention wavers and gently guiding it back to the conversation. It's about acknowledging the pull of digital devices and the meandering of your thoughts and consciously refocusing on the person before you. By doing so, you're carving out a space where distractions have less power, and the genuine exchange of ideas, emotions, and stories can flourish.

In the journey of active listening, obstacles will hinder your progress. The noise within your mind, distractions from the digital realm, and wandering thoughts disrupt your connection with your loved ones. Armed with mindfulness and conscious attention, you can navigate these obstacles and clear a path to deeper understanding and meaningful conversations. So, take a moment to acknowledge the noise, turn off the phone, step away from the computer and the magazine, silence your wandering thoughts, embrace the transformative power of focused listening, and pave the way for more fulfilling connections.

Your Wish to Help

The impulse to offer well-intentioned advice to our loved ones often arises from a place of genuine concern and care. We want to alleviate their problems and guide them toward solutions because we believe it will benefit them. However, this natural instinct can sometimes hinder the practice of active listening. When we rush to provide advice or solutions, we may inadvertently divert the focus from the speaker's emotions and experiences to our own perspectives. In doing so, we risk invalidating their feelings, dismissing their concerns, or making them feel unheard. Active listening, on the other hand, involves creating a space where the speaker can freely express themselves, share their thoughts and emotions without interruption or judgment. It requires setting aside our impulse to provide solutions and instead immersing ourselves in their world, truly understanding their point of view. By prioritizing empathy and understanding over advice-giving, we can foster deeper connections and support our loved ones more effectively in the long run.

Thinking in Terms of Right and Wrong

There is a saying that many authors and speakers have used to emphasize the danger that thinking in terms of right and wrong can have on our relationships: "Do you want to be right, or do you want to be happy." The saying illustrates that thinking in terms of right and wrong introduces a judgmental element that can undermine the genuine understanding and empathy active listening seeks to foster. When we approach a conversation with a preconceived notion of what is right or wrong, we tend to filter information through this rigid framework, leading us to evaluate the speaker's words based on our own beliefs and values. This bias can impede our ability to appreciate the speaker's perspective fully, as we may be quick to dismiss or discount their viewpoint if it differs from our own. Active listening, on the contrary, necessitates a suspension of judgment, creating a safe and open space where the speaker can express themselves without fear of condemnation. It involves embracing the idea that people have diverse experiences and opinions, and the goal is not to establish who is right or wrong but to understand the emotions, thoughts, and needs underlying their words.

Chapter 4: Exercises to Deepen Your Listening Skills and Strengthen Your Connection

Welcome to the heart of your adventure as you become an attentive listener and cultivate a deeper, more meaningful connection with your loved one. The following exercises aren't about rushing through a to-do list, but rather, they're invitations to dive into moments of thoughtful engagement with the world around you. So, set forth on this journey, one step at a time.

Practicing new skills is where the rubber meets the road in any personal development journey. It's the bridge between theory and reality, where knowledge transforms into tangible change. This transformation occurs through the repetition and application of what you've learned, turning abstract concepts into ingrained behaviors.

In the context of becoming a more attentive listener and nurturing deeper connections, practicing these skills is paramount. While understanding the importance of active listening is valuable, it's the consistent application of this understanding that will revolutionize your relationships.

Consider it akin to learning to play a musical instrument or mastering a sport. You can study theory, read books, and watch videos, but true proficiency only comes from practice. It's the hours spent playing scales or shooting free throws that turn an amateur into a virtuoso or an athlete into a champion. Similarly, honing your listening skills through practice will elevate your ability to connect with your loved ones.

Furthermore, practicing these skills not only benefits you but also demonstrates your commitment to your relationships. When your loved ones see your consistent effort to be a better listener, they're more likely to reciprocate, fostering a positive feedback loop of improved communication and understanding.

So, embrace this journey of attentive listening as an ongoing practice. It's not about perfection but progress. As you consistently apply these skills, you'll find that your relationships become more profound, fulfilling, and enriched with the authenticity that comes from truly being present for those you cherish.

Additionally, keeping a journal or jotting down your thoughts, reflections, ideas, and plans while working through these exercises in Chapter 4 can significantly enhance your growth. Writing provides a tangible record of your progress, helping you track your journey from theory to practical application. It serves as a valuable tool for self-awareness, allowing you to revisit and refine your insights, ultimately deepening your listening skills and strengthening your connections. It's a compass that guides you through the intricacies of your personal development voyage, ensuring that your path remains purposeful and transformative.

Exercise 1: Reflect on Your Listening Style

Pause and read the questions below, taking time for them to sink in before you answer them. Take time to contemplate your usual listening patterns and inclinations, and don't hold back—the more honest you are, the more progress you will make. If you are an awful listener, you must acknowledge it before you become an excellent listener.

Consider discussing the questions with a close friend or loved one to seek their perspective. As you gather their input, approach it with an open mind, setting aside defensiveness. Embrace a spirit of curiosity and gain more understanding.

Questions:

1. In conversations, do I sometimes respond to emails or messages on my phone?

2. Do I try to create a comforting atmosphere when faced with sensitive topics?

3. Do I find myself giving advice even when it hasn't been sought?

4. Do I tend to complete other people's sentences?

5. Am I more focused on what I want to say next rather than listening?

6. Do I easily get distracted by my surroundings during conversations?

7. Do I often make judgments or assign interpretations to the words being said?

What Is the Benefit of Doing This Exercise?

Self-reflection is a powerful tool that not only unveils your listening habits but also offers a multitude of benefits that extend beyond merely understanding your inclinations. First and foremost, self-reflection serves as a vital stepping stone toward enhanced active listening. By shedding light on your default listening behaviors, you gain valuable insights into areas where improvement is needed. This heightened awareness empowers you to actively address and refine your listening skills.

However, the advantages of self-reflection don't stop there. It serves as the cornerstone for a broader journey of self-awareness. As you delve into your listening style, you'll likely uncover patterns and tendencies that extend into other aspects of your life. Recognizing these parallels can trigger a profound personal transformation, where you become more attuned not only to how you listen but also to how you interact, communicate, and connect with others.

"I thought I was a decent listener, but after doing this exercise, I realized I'm impatient. I don't wait for people around me to finish talking; I regularly interrupt. It helped me become more aware and patient in conversations, even if it's challenging." - Brad, 42

Exercise 2: Practice Empathetic Reflections

Over the next couple of days, study the people around you. Observe and contemplate the viewpoints of those you cross paths with, whether they're familiar faces, friends, or strangers, and try to envision life from their unique perspective.

Questions:

1. What is effortless for them?
2. What trials could they be navigating?
3. What do you think are their needs, fears, and dreams?
4. What resonates in their actions, and what doesn't?

Remember, this is a guessing game. The precision of your insights matters less than the sincere intent to empathize. As you engage in this practice, write down your thoughts and discoveries in your journal. What revelations caught you by surprise? What lessons did you glean from stepping into someone else's shoes?

What Is the Benefit of Doing This Exercise?

This exercise cultivates your empathy and amplifies your ability to comprehend others. As you hone your capacity to grasp someone else's outlook, you lay the groundwork for compassionate listening. This deepened curiosity and willingness to embrace diverse viewpoints will inevitably pave the way for more prosperous and profound interactions.

"I'm a middle-grade school teacher. I practiced this exercise with my colleagues, the children I teach, and my partner. I even tried it with characters in a TV show I watch.

It was challenging at first, but it became something I genuinely enjoyed. I noticed it helped me be present when my partner shared her day or concerns. A fantastic exercise!" - Layla, 29

Exercise 3: Create a Distraction-Free Environment

This exercise is a mini-ritual for meaningful conversations. Before conversing with your loved one, create an environment that minimizes distractions. Turn off your phone, computer, and TV. If possible, close the door or let other family members know you need a few moments of focused attention. During the conversation, maintain eye contact and resist the urge to multitask. This is your dedicated time to listen with attention. Now answer the following questions.

Questions:

1. What else can I do to create a distraction-free environment?
2. How will I handle interruptions during our conversation?
3. What strategies can I use to stay attentive and engaged?
4. Are there any steps I should take before starting this exercise, such as setting an intention or ensuring I'm comfortable?

What Is the Benefit of Doing This Exercise?

When you sweep aside external distractions and curate an environment tailor-made for heartfelt listening, something magical happens. You're saying, "You matter to me," in a language that needs no words. Dedicating your undivided attention sends ripples of connection and trust into the air, deepening the bonds between you and your loved one.

"This exercise was particularly impactful during serious conversations with my wife. I'm usually buried in work-related tasks, making it easy to be distracted by my phone or computer. However, turning everything off allowed me to focus on her. I could sense her relaxation and trust in my newfound attentiveness. It felt like a breath of fresh air in our long-standing marriage." - Charles, 57

Exercise 4: Practice Empathetic Body Language

As you engage in conversations, make a mindful effort to infuse empathetic body language cues. These small yet impactful gestures enhance your connection with others. Here's your trio of cues: the nod, the genuine smile, and the subtle lean-in. Picture yourself occasionally nodding as the other person speaks. It's as if your nods are gentle affirmations, reassuring them that their words are being heard and understood. Nod, just enough that they know you are listening but not so much that it looks like you are agreeing with every word.

Wear a genuine smile. Offer this heartfelt expression as if you're not just sharing a smile but sharing warmth, acceptance, and a genuine interest in what's being said.

Lastly, the subtle lean-in. Lean in just a touch, as if you're leaning into their world. This movement signifies your undivided attention and creates an intimate atmosphere.

Incorporating these cues isn't about scripted actions. It's about weaving a natural symphony of connection. So, remember to nod, smile, and lean in the next time you're engaged in conversation.

What Is the Benefit of Doing This Exercise?

Instead of just hearing your partner's words, you're using a secret language of empathy through your body. Now and then, a nod of understanding or agreement lets them know you're physically and mentally there. And then there's the power of a genuine smile. A genuine grin says, "I'm here with you, and I care about what you're saying." It's a warm embrace for their words. And if you're leaning in a bit, it shows you're fully present and intrigued by every word. These gestures might seem small, but they're magical ingredients that make a regular conversation a special connection.

"I realized how much of a difference these small gestures made in conversations. When I nodded and smiled while my partner talked about her day, he seemed more open and at ease. It was like a silent reassurance that I was truly there with him." - Max, 35

Exercise 5: Listen Patiently and Avoid Interrupting

In this exercise, you're on a mission to master the art of patience and presence. Imagine being in a conversation where your instinct to jump in with your thoughts takes a backseat. Your task is simple yet profound: let the speaker have the stage until they've poured out their thoughts.

It might feel like a gentle battle against impatience, but fear not, for you hold the power of deep breaths. When you feel that restlessness tugging at you, take a moment to inhale and exhale. It's a mini reset button for your focus. These breaths become your anchor, grounding you in the here and now, ensuring that every word is received with the respect it deserves.

As you embark on this journey, remember it's not about suppressing your eagerness to contribute. It's about allowing the other person's words to take center stage. It's a dance of conversation where you let them lead and follow their rhythm. So, let the words flow, and when the time comes for your response, you'll find it's infused with a deeper understanding born from patient listening.

Now, answer the following questions:

1. What other techniques can I use to practice patience?

2. How will I know when it's time for me to jump in and share my thoughts?

3. What strategies can I use to focus on the speaker's words during a conversation?

4. Is there anything else I should remember while engaging in this exercise?

What Is the Benefit of Doing This Exercise?

By patiently allowing the speaker to convey their thoughts uninterrupted, you're opening a doorway to a more profound connection. Patient listening becomes a bridge that spans between hearts, fostering a sense of trust and mutual respect. As you let their words settle within you, you absorb the essence of their thoughts. This absorption becomes the key to a deeper level of understanding, where you take the time to contemplate things and let your words carry that weight in reply.

"Practicing patience in conversations was really really difficult for me but surprisingly enlightening. I realized that my habit of interrupting was a hindrance to meaningful discussions. When I truly listened without interrupting, I gained a more profound insight into my husband's viewpoint. It felt like a respectful exchange of ideas." - Emily, 28

Exercise 6: Don't Give Unwanted Advice

You have someone telling you about a problem they're facing. It could be your partner, your colleague, or a friend. Even though you want to help, advising without them asking can cause conflict; instead, you're going to try something different.

When your friend talks to you about something, try not to jump in with advice right away. Instead, be like a good listener. Pay attention to what they're saying, and show that you care about their feelings. You can nod or say things like "I understand" or "That must be tough."

Now, here's the exciting part. Toward the end of your conversation, you can ask your friend if they want to hear your thoughts or advice about what they shared. "Do you need any help or advice?" This way, you let them decide if they're ready to hear your ideas.

What Is the Benefit of Doing This Exercise?

Resisting the urge to offer unsolicited advice creates an open space for deeper understanding in your interactions. It's akin to establishing a unique zone where you honor their autonomy, allowing them to steer the conversation. This approach fosters genuine dialogue and often empowers them to uncover their own solutions. Sometimes, simply articulating thoughts can be the key to finding a way forward. At other times, people just need an outlet to express their feelings, and sharing the problem becomes the solution.

By refraining from immediate advice-giving, you uncover the core of their concerns, much like peeling the layers of an onion to reach its juicy center. This process offers a comprehensive understanding of their situation and enables you to provide tailored guidance if and when they seek it.

Your willingness to listen without imposing advice enriches your connection and empowers them to navigate their challenges effectively.

"This exercise shifted my approach entirely. I used to jump in with advice, thinking I was helping. But when I held back and listened without immediately offering solutions, I saw how much more willing my partner was to share. It allowed us to have conversations that felt truly collaborative." - Alex, 41

Exercise 7: Ask Three Open-Ended Questions

Embrace the art of using open-ended questions – these are special tools that help conversations blossom into something deeper and more meaningful. Your loved one is sharing with you—it could be a story, thought, or something they're worried about. Before you jump in with your thoughts or advice, make it a habit to ask them at least three questions that can't be answered with a simple "yes" or "no." These questions are little invitations for them to share even more. You unravel a mystery together, step by step, and gain more understanding of what they are conveying.

Your partner is telling you about a challenging situation at work. Instead of jumping in with advice or sharing a similar experience, you might ask:

"How did you feel when that happened?"

"What were the main factors that led to the situation?"

"So, how did you finally address the issue?"

What Is the Benefit of Doing This Exercise?

As you sprinkle these open-ended questions into conversations, you'll notice something extraordinary happening. The person you're talking to will feel like you're genuinely interested in what they're saying. In short, you're giving them a front-row seat to share their thoughts and feelings. It's like being a detective, where your questions uncover hidden treasures of insight and emotion. You create a dialogue that showcases your genuine interest and curiosity by incorporating open-ended questions.

"I'll admit, this exercise felt awkward at first. But I decided to try it not only with my partner but also with my teenage daughter and colleagues at work. When my partner mentioned having a terrible day, instead of swiftly moving on to my own stories, I asked her more about her experience. It led to an unexpectedly profound conversation. I discovered her anxieties about her new position and her fear of failure. It was a conversation that helped both of us in ways I hadn't anticipated." - Amir, 38

Exercise 8: Mirroring

In deeper conversations, like when your loved one opens up about their worries or concerns, give mirroring a try. Take a moment to repeat or rephrase some of the keywords or phrases they've used. This isn't about simply parroting back their words. It's about capturing the essence of what they're saying thoughtfully and meaningfully. For instance, if your loved one says, "I've been feeling overwhelmed with work lately," you might respond with something like, "It sounds like your job has been causing a lot of stress." This simple reflection lets them know that you're truly listening and trying to grasp the emotions they're experiencing.

Here's an exercise to help you practice. Start a conversation with your loved one, and then try mirroring some of the words they use during the talk.

What Is the Benefit of Doing This Exercise?

Mirroring is a tool that shows you're participating in a conversation. It does a lot of good things. First of all, it shows you're paying close attention and genuinely trying to understand the other person. Secondly, it helps your partner think more deeply about their thoughts and feelings, making the conversation more meaningful. Also, mirroring helps your loved one think about what they've said. Finally, this tool makes the conversation feel open and honest, letting both people connect in a more authentic and honest way.

"I was intrigued by the idea of mirroring, and when I tried it, the impact was profound. As my partner shared her worries about her career, I repeated a few of her phrases. I saw her pause, reflect, and then continue to share even more. It felt like I was giving her the space to explore her thoughts, and it deepened our connection." -Mark, 29

Exercise 9: Focus on Non-Verbal Cues

As you engage in conversations, take a deliberate step back from the words spoken and direct your focus toward the non-verbal cues. They reveal a treasure trove of emotions and thoughts that often remain unspoken.

As you immerse yourself in this practice, pay close attention to your partner's subtle body language. Notice how they move, stand, or use their hands while talking. Catch the play of expressions across their face, from the raise of an eyebrow to the curve of a smile. Listen not just to the words but to their voice's cadence, pitch, and intonation. These factors contribute to the hidden layers of meaning beneath the surface.

Write down some of the non-verbal cues you noticed in your conversations.

- Facial expressions (smiles, frowns, raised eyebrows)

- Posture and gestures (leaning forward, arms crossed)

- Vocal intonation (low voice, loud voice, excited tone)

- Eye contact (direct, averted)

What Is the Benefit of Doing This Exercise?

These non-verbal cues add depth and dimension to the spoken words. They communicate excitement, hesitation, confidence, or uncertainty. They provide insights into the speaker's state of mind that words alone might not convey. It's a skillful art of decoding the unspoken and tuning in to the unsaid, and it holds the potential to transform your conversations into something profound. During active listening, you can simply note these cues or use them to reflect back, saying,

"You seem concerned; how do you feel?" or "You look really happy."
This demonstrates empathy.

By honing your ability to interpret these subtle cues, you're opening
yourself up to a richer understanding of the person you're conversing
with. You're peeling back the layers, delving beneath the surface, and
connecting on a deeper level. This exercise isn't just about what's
being said; it's about delving into the unspoken, embracing the full
spectrum of human communication. So, in your following
conversation, let your attention linger on these non-verbal cues, and
watch as a whole new world of connection unfolds before you.

Tuning into non-verbal cues enhances your listening prowess in
numerous ways:

- You gain insight into your loved one's emotions, allowing
  you to respond with greater sensitivity
- Your presence and attentiveness are heightened, fostering
  an environment of trust and understanding
- Your ability to connect on a deeper level expands as you
  acknowledge the unspoken aspects of communication
- Misunderstandings are minimized as you're attuned to the
  full spectrum of their expression

*"Shifting my focus to non-verbal cues felt like discovering a hidden
language. When my partner recounted a challenging experience, I
noticed the tension in her shoulders and the vulnerability in her
voice. It allowed me to respond in a way that addressed both the
words she spoke and the emotions she conveyed." - Lisa, 33*

Exercise 10: Practice Gratitude

Incorporate a touch of gratitude into the fabric of your conversations, weaving a thread of appreciation that enhances the connection you share.

So, when your loved one opens up and shares their thoughts or feelings, take a moment to say thanks. It's a way of showing them you value their honesty and trust. Sometimes, they might hold back, thinking they're burdening you with their worries. Gratitude can reassure them that you're grateful they're sharing.

What Is the Benefit of Doing This Exercise?

This practice is a gentle pause in the flow of your conversation. It's a moment where you intentionally step back and recognize the significance of what is unfolding. As your partner shares their world with you, you take a moment to let them know how much you value their honesty and trust. It's like adding a sprinkle of gratitude that encourage your loved one to continue opening up.

This act of gratitude not only brings warmth to the conversation but also serves as a bridge of connection. It's a way of saying, "I see you, I hear you, and I appreciate you." In this simple gesture, you're fostering mutual respect and understanding.

Practicing gratitude enriches your interactions in remarkable ways:

- Your loved one feels acknowledged and valued, creating a safe space for authentic sharing
- Gratitude fosters a positive and affirming atmosphere, elevating the quality of your conversations
- It encourages reciprocal gratitude, creating a cycle of appreciation that strengthens your bond

- The practice of gratitude enriches your perspective and mindset, contributing to a more fulfilling relationship

So, the next time your loved one opens up to you, remember to pause and let gratitude fill the air. Your words of thanks might be brief, but their impact has the potential to leave both of you with a connection and positivity.

"Incorporating gratitude into our conversations was a game-changer. When my partner opened up about a personal challenge, I took a moment to thank her for her honesty and trust. The warmth in her smile and the gratitude she expressed back to me made me realize how such a simple act can uplift the entire interaction." - David, 46

These exercises act as doorways to stronger connections, nurturing understanding, empathy, and gratitude. With each exercise, you work toward active listening, enhancing the relationships that hold great significance.

Chapter 5: Active Listening Beyond Romantic Relationships

You've delved into the transformative power of active listening within the context of romantic relationships. You've explored how this simple yet profound skill deepens connections, fosters understanding, and cultivates partner trust. But the beauty of active listening extends far beyond romantic love—it's a tool that has the potential to enhance every facet of your life where interaction and communication thrive.

Think about your interactions with friends, colleagues, clients, children, neighbors, and casual acquaintances. In each encounter, the ability to listen shapes the dynamics of your relationships and contributes to a more harmonious and fulfilling existence. Active listening isn't confined to romantic intimacy. It's a universal language that has the power to transcend boundaries and break down barriers. It can also bridge gaps between individuals from all walks of life.

As you continue your active listening journey, you'll explore how it serves as a cornerstone of relationships. You'll uncover its significance in friendships, where the bonds of camaraderie are strengthened through genuine engagement. You'll venture into the professional realm, where active listening catalyzes success. You'll delve into the intricate dynamics of parent-child relationships, discovering how active listening nurtures trust and openness with the youngest members of society.

But the journey doesn't stop there. You'll also unearth the magic of active listening in everyday interactions, from engaging with acquaintances to fostering a sense of unity within communities. You'll uncover how this practice, when applied with intention and care, has the potential to transform your relationships and yourself. Through active listening, you will become more attuned to your emotions and expand your horizons.

Active Listening with Friends

In the tapestry of your life, friendships are the vibrant threads that weave together moments of joy, laughter, and shared experiences. You only need to think about your friends to conjure up rich memories and emotions. Friends offer solace in times of need and an anchor to your sense of belonging. While active listening is often associated with romantic relationships, its significance in friendships should not be underestimated.

The Role of Active Listening in Friendships

You sit across from a close friend in a cafe. The aroma of freshly brewed coffee fills the air, and the conversation flows effortlessly. As your friend shares their thoughts, aspirations, and worries, you immerse yourself in their words, fully present in the moment. This act of tuning into their story without the distractions of your thoughts or preconceptions is the essence of active listening.

Active listening in friendships goes beyond the surface-level exchange of information. It involves creating a safe space where your friend feels heard, valued, and understood. By focusing on the meaning behind their words, you show your interest and investment in their feelings. This simple yet profound act sets the stage for deeper connections and emotional support.

Building Stronger Connections and Emotional Support

Active listening is the cornerstone of meaningful friendships. When you lend your ear with empathy and intent, you extend an unspoken invitation for your friend to share their innermost thoughts and emotions without judgment. Through active listening, you offer a shoulder to lean on, strengthening your bond and creating a reciprocal cycle of trust and vulnerability. When your friend feels heard, they're more likely to reciprocate, and you benefit more from the exchange.

Avoiding Misunderstandings and Conflicts

Misunderstandings and conflicts mar even the most steadfast friendships. Often, these arise from misinterpreted words or unexpressed feelings. Active listening acts as a guardian against these pitfalls. It allows you to decode the unspoken messages beneath your friend's words.

Your friend mentions a seemingly inconsequential disappointment. Through active listening, you discern the undercurrent of hurt behind their words. It prompts you to delve deeper into their emotions. By gently probing and asking open-ended questions, you uncover the source of their distress and offer a compassionate space for them to heal.

Personal Anecdotes and Examples

As a dedicated, active listener, Sarah vividly recalls a conversation with her friend Alex. He had been acting distant lately, and Sarah sensed something was amiss. She practiced active listening over a cup of tea, allowing Alex to open up at his own pace. As he shared his concerns about work-related stress, Sarah nodded empathetically and asked questions that invited him to elaborate. When he felt heard and not judged, he opened up about how his rejection for a promotion reminded him of previous romantic rejections and old feelings were stirred. Alex felt a weight lifted off his shoulders through this dialogue, and their friendship emerged stronger than before.

Similarly, active listening was pivotal in Dave's friendship with Mia. When Mia faced a crossroads in her career, Dave's attentive presence during their conversations allowed her to explore her fears and aspirations. He did not offer solutions, and by Mia talking through what she really wanted from life, she was able to decide on a career option she was not initially considering. Dave's unwavering support and genuine interest emboldened Mia to pursue a new path, and their friendship became a pillar of strength throughout her journey.

In the realm of friendships, active listening is the bridge that spans the gap between hearts. By embracing this practice, you become a confidant, supporter, and architect of enduring connections that weather the test of time.

Active Listening with Colleagues and Clients

In the bustling landscape of your professional life, effective communication is the compass that guides you toward success. While technical skills and expertise are crucial, active listening is a powerful tool for dealing with colleagues and clients.

Enhancing Communication in Professional Settings

You are in a dynamic brainstorming session where ideas ricochet off the walls, each participant eager to contribute. Amid this vibrant exchange, active listening acts as a stabilizing force. By attentively absorbing your colleagues' insights and perspectives, you breathe life into their words and foster mutual respect. As you engage in active listening, you pave the way for more transparent communication, ensuring that each voice is heard and valued.

This does not mean that you don't voice your opinion. You must first listen to others (and hope they listen to you), so you can understand how your ideas will fit the preconceptions and opinions of others. If your boss wants to eliminate video calls in favor of emails, you are unlikely to find sympathy for your idea of a weekly team call.

In meetings, negotiations, and even casual water-cooler conversations, active listening is a bridge that transcends hierarchies and titles. It encourages open dialogue and paves the way for creative solutions. As colleagues witness your dedication to listening, they're more likely to reciprocate—it creates a synergy that propels the team forward.

Fostering Effective Teamwork and Collaboration

In the intricate dance of collaboration, active listening takes center stage as the choreographer of seamless teamwork. By hearing your colleagues' ideas, concerns, and aspirations, you lay the foundation for shared goals and collective success. This practice of empathy fuels a spirit of cooperation. It enables team members to blend their unique strengths harmoniously.

Consider a project where diverse perspectives converge. Through active listening, you unearth the wisdom that each team member brings to the table. By valuing their insights and integrating them into the project's framework, you not only enhance the outcome but also nurture a sense of ownership and camaraderie among your colleagues.

Active listening negates lousy communication. If you take the words at face value, you will miss the true intent of the comment. Listen to what your co-workers want beyond what they ask for.

Building Rapport with Clients and Improving Customer Relationships

Beyond the office walls, active listening extends its embrace to the world of clients and customers. Every interaction becomes an opportunity to create an experience that resonates, leaving a lasting impression. Whether you're an entrepreneur, a sales professional, or a customer service representative, active listening elevates your interactions to personalized connections.

A client expresses frustration with a product's functionality. Through active listening, you delve into the layers of their dissatisfaction. You understand the technical glitch and also the emotional toll it has taken. Acknowledging their concerns and showing genuine empathy transforms a challenging situation into a testament to exceptional customer service. They might be frustrated with broader issues that are not connected to your product, and by listening to them, you can refocus on how your product, or other products, will help.

Active Listening in Parent-Child Relationships

Parenting is woven with love, guidance, and connection. Amid the laughter, questions, and challenges, active listening emerges as a potent thread that binds parent and child in a cocoon of understanding and trust.

Strengthening the Parent-Child Bond through Active Listening

A child's eyes light up as they recount their day, eager to share every detail. By embracing active listening, you pave the way for a deeper connection that enriches the parent-child bond. Through your undivided attention and genuine curiosity, you signal to your child that their words hold immense value. This affirmation nurtures a sense of security and belonging, cultivating a bond that weathers the storms of adolescence and beyond. It is not about the individual acts but the emotions they want to share with you.

Creating a Safe and Open Environment for Children to Share

In active listening, your role as a parent transforms into that of a confidant. You create a safe haven where vulnerability is celebrated by carving out moments to listen attentively to your child's triumphs and tribulations. As they navigate the maze of emotions and experiences, your unwavering presence fosters a sense of acceptance. It emboldens them to share even their deepest fears and dreams.

Teaching Empathy and Communication Skills to Children

The gift of active listening extends far beyond parent-child conversations. It plants the seeds of empathy and effective communication in your child's heart. As you model the art of active listening, you impart a valuable life skill that empowers them to connect authentically with others throughout life. Through your example, they learn that listening isn't just about hearing words; it's about understanding emotions, validating experiences, and fostering connections.

Your child recounts a challenging encounter at school. Your attentive listening validates their feelings. It teaches them the art of empathetic engagement. As you ask questions that delve deeper into their experience, you equip them with the tools to navigate similar situations with empathy and grace.

Balancing Active Listening with Guidance and Discipline

The harmony of active listening lies in its dance with guidance and discipline. As a parent, you don multiple hats, including that of a listener, a mentor, and a guide. While active listening nurtures openness, it doesn't negate your role in providing guidance and setting boundaries. It's within this delicate balance that the true essence of active listening flourishes.

Consider when your child confides in you about a mistake they've made. Through active listening, you create an environment where they feel safe to share their misstep. As the conversation unfolds, your guidance and wisdom gently steer them toward understanding the consequences and learning from their actions.

Active Listening in Everyday Interactions

Active listening isn't confined to intimate relationships alone. It unfurls its magic in everyday interactions. It weaves threads of connection that span across communities and cultures.

Utilizing Active Listening in Various Situations

Picture a warm exchange with a neighbor as you discuss the garden or chat about local events. You listen as they share their stories, laughing and nodding with understanding. Even in these seemingly casual conversations, active listening plays a pivotal role. By attentively engaging in discussions, you create an atmosphere of authenticity that transcends superficiality. Whether it's a brief encounter with an acquaintance or a heart-to-heart with a close friend, the principles of active listening remain steadfast.

Building a Supportive and Compassionate Community

Your interactions with neighbors, co-workers, and fellow community members form the vibrant pieces that shape your sense of belonging. When woven into these interactions, active listening nurtures the foundation of a supportive and compassionate community. A community where each individual feels heard and understood is a community that thrives—a community where people support others. A space is created where diverse voices find resonance by engaging in active listening. In no time, you'll be forging connections beyond the surface and extending to a place of shared humanity.

Acknowledging Diverse Perspectives and Backgrounds

In conversations with individuals from varied backgrounds, cultures, and experiences, active listening serves as a bridge that connects differences. Through empathetic engagement, you honor and validate the unique stories and viewpoints that each person brings to the table. This recognition fosters an environment where inclusivity thrives. It nurtures a sense of unity amidst diversity.

The Ripple Effect of Active Listening on Overall Well-being

The significance of active listening transcends singular moments. It ripples outward, shaping individual interactions and your overall well-being. Think about a day when you engaged in multiple interactions where active listening was the cornerstone. What did you learn from others? How connected did you feel with those people? It's like you felt more connected than you did to your bus driver or the person who scanned your groceries, and all because active listening created a connection. Connection anchors you in the present and enriches your relationship with the world around you—it touches the core of your being and fosters a profound sense of interconnectedness.

Active Listening and Personal Growth

Active listening extends beyond being a mere bridge-builder among individuals; it acts as a catalyst propelling personal growth and self-exploration.

Active Listening and Personal Development

The willingness to embrace new perspectives and experiences is at the heart of personal growth. Active listening is a cornerstone for this growth, guiding you toward a deeper understanding of yourself and others. As you actively engage with the stories and thoughts of those around you, you embark on a path of self-improvement that extends far beyond the surface.

Developing Self-Awareness and Emotional Intelligence

Active listening isn't confined to understanding external narratives; it also invites you to delve into the recesses of your minds and hearts. You cultivate a heightened sense of self-awareness by honing your ability to listen attentively. This self-awareness acts as a mirror, reflecting your thoughts, emotions, and biases, and enables you to navigate your inner landscape with greater clarity.

Active listening nurtures emotional intelligence. It's a vital skill that empowers you to comprehend and manage your emotions while also empathizing with the feelings of others. You fine-tune your emotional radar through this practice, fostering richer and more meaningful connections.

Learning from Others' Experiences and Viewpoints

Every person you encounter carries a bag of experiences interwoven with lessons and insights. By lending an attentive ear, you open yourself to the wisdom others offer. Whether it's a friend sharing their triumphs and tribulations or a colleague recounting their professional journey, active listening transforms you into an eager learner who absorbs the nuances that life has bestowed upon others.

When you listen to the stories of others, you find the seeds of personal growth, gleaning knowledge from the narratives of those who have walked different paths. Their experiences become your guideposts, illuminating the way forward and offering fresh perspectives on your life.

You engage in a heartfelt conversation with someone from a different culture or background and step into their shoes through active listening, momentarily experiencing life from their vantage point. This expansion of worldview fosters empathy by deepening your understanding of different cultures, lifestyles, beliefs, and realities.

As you conclude your exploration into the art of active listening, you'll find yourself equipped with a versatile tool that transcends the boundaries of relationships, professions, and everyday interactions.

Active listening strengthens connections that bind you, from friends to colleagues, parents to children, and even the interactions with those you barely know. It breathes life into conversations, transforming them from mere exchanges of words into meaningful dialogues that nourish your soul.

At the core of active listening lies the fundamental truth that it nurtures trust and understanding, building bridges over chasms of miscommunication. It fosters an environment where misunderstandings struggle to take root.

Chapter 6: Embracing a Lifetime of Active Listening

Congratulations! You're nearing the completion of this book. Your dedication and commitment to enhancing your communication skills and deepening your connections with loved ones deserve applause. As you reflect on the journey you've embarked upon, take a moment to acknowledge the progress you've made and the insights you've gained.

Throughout this workbook, you've delved into the art of active listening. It's a skill that transforms relationships and nurtures profound connections. By immersing yourself in the exercises and principles outlined within these pages, you've taken significant steps toward becoming a more empathetic, attuned, and compassionate listener.

In a world often characterized by distractions and hurried exchanges, your decision to engage with this workbook speaks volumes about your commitment to meaningful communication. You've ventured beyond the surface of conversations and embraced the depths of dialogue where proper understanding and genuine connection flourish.

Yet, your journey doesn't end here. It's only the beginning. This workbook has provided you with a solid foundation, a toolkit with insights and strategies to support your active listening journey. And just like any skill worth mastering, active listening requires continuous practice and application in all facets of life.

As you turn the pages ahead, you'll discover the final exercise, a personal plan for being an active listener for life. Here, you'll be able to reflect upon your experiences with this workbook and create strategies for incorporating active listening into your everyday routines.

Summary of Active Listening Principles

Active listening is a dynamic and empathetic way of engaging with others that fosters understanding, trust, and connection. Throughout your journey in the Shut Up and Listen workbook, you've delved into five essential principles that form the bedrock of active listening. Here's a recap and distillation of these principles—each of these is a vital component in your quest to become a more attentive and compassionate listener.

Pay Attention: The Art of Undistracted Focus

In a world of distractions, giving your undivided attention is a profound gesture of respect and presence. You create a space where meaningful conversations can unfold by consciously avoiding diversions, such as checking your phone or letting your mind wander. This principle underlines the importance of prioritizing the speaker and embracing the power of focused engagement.

Show Interest: Nurturing Connections through Nonverbal Cues

Nonverbal cues play a significant role in communication, often speaking louder than words. By maintaining eye contact, nodding, or using other gestures that convey engagement, you signal to the speaker that their words are valued and heard—you are paying attention. These subtle signals create an environment of trust and openness, encouraging the speaker to share more authentically.

Clarify: Seeking Clarity for Accurate Understanding

Asking clarifying questions is a cornerstone of active listening, ensuring you accurately grasp the speaker's intended message. By seeking clarification, you validate their words and demonstrate a genuine commitment to comprehending their perspective. This principle emphasizes the importance of curiosity and the willingness to delve deeper into the speaker's thoughts.

Reflect: Echoing Understanding through Paraphrasing

Mirroring the speaker's words through paraphrasing is a robust validation of their thoughts and feelings. Summarizing and echoing their statements showcases your attentive listening and affirms that you comprehend their message. This principle deepens the connection by revealing your investment in understanding their viewpoint.

Empathize: Connecting on an Emotional Level

Empathy forms the heart of active listening, allowing you to understand the speaker's words and acknowledge and resonate with their emotions. By showing empathy, you create a safe space for the speaker to express their feelings, fostering deeper connection and understanding.

As you revisit these active listening principles, remember that they intertwine and complement each other, enhancing your ability to engage authentically with others. The foundation you've laid through these principles equips you to navigate conversations with greater intention, sensitivity, and depth. By incorporating these principles into your interactions, you embark on a journey of building trust, fostering empathy, and creating enriching relationships.

Embracing a Lifetime of Active Listening

You've delved into the art of active listening and discovered its transformative impact on your relationships. As you complete this book, you must recognize that active listening is not merely a chapter in your life; it's a lifelong journey that enriches your interactions, personal growth, and self-awareness.

Expanding the Scope of Active Listening

While this book has mainly focused on fostering active listening within the context of your relationships, the principles you've learned extend far beyond those boundaries. Embracing active listening as a lifelong practice invites you to apply it to various aspects of your life. Whether you're conversing with friends, colleagues, acquaintances, or even engaging in public discourse, active listening can create meaningful connections and bridge understanding, and the basics remain the same for every type of connection.

Enhancing Relationships and Communication

Active listening forms the bedrock of successful relationships by nurturing trust, empathy, and open communication. By perpetually cultivating the art of listening, you empower yourself to forge deeper connections with your loved ones, colleagues, and new acquaintances. Through attentive listening, you validate others' experiences, making them feel valued and understood. This potent tool minimizes misunderstandings, resolves conflicts, and paves the way for harmonious interactions.

The Role of Active Listening in Personal Growth and Self-Awareness

Beyond its impact on relationships, active listening plays a pivotal role in your personal development journey. You expand your horizons and challenge preconceived notions by actively engaging with diverse perspectives. Through empathetic listening, you gain insight into the emotions and experiences of others, broadening your understanding of the human experience. It enhances your emotional intelligence and fosters a heightened self-awareness as you reflect on your responses and reactions during conversations.

By nurturing active listening as an integral part of your life, you embark on a journey of continuous growth and self-improvement. The skills you've acquired within these pages lay the foundation for enriching your interactions and deepening your connections to cultivate a more compassionate, empathetic way of engaging with the world around you. Something to be proud of!

Your Last Exercise: Your Plan for Lifelong Active Listening

Congratulations! It's finally time to unveil the last exercise in this book. To ensure that you maintain the valuable skills you've acquired, you will create a personalized plan for daily active listening.

Before you dive into practical strategies, take a moment to acknowledge that active listening is an ongoing endeavor. Just like any skill, it requires consistent practice and dedication. As you progress, remind yourself that each interaction presents an opportunity to grow as an active listener and strengthen your relationships. It's time to implement practical strategies to weave active listening into your daily routine.

Set a Daily Intention for Active Listening

Active listening begins with intention. Each morning, take a few moments to set your intention for the day: to prioritize active listening in your interactions. For example, if you have a morning meeting scheduled, you might intend to actively listen to your colleague's ideas without interrupting. So your daily intention would look like "Today, I will actively listen to my colleague during our morning meeting, giving them my full attention and refraining from interrupting."

Now, take a few moments to develop your daily intention for active listening in your journal or notebook. Repeat each morning.

Using Visual Cues to Refocus During Conversations

Visual cues serve as powerful reminders to stay present during conversations. Choose a small object or symbol (like a colored wristband) and place it where you'll see it often. When you see it, pause and refocus on the person you're listening to. For instance, you might wear the wristband on your non-dominant hand as a reminder to actively listen. Your visual cue would be, "I will place a blue wristband on my left wrist and use it as a reminder to be present and attentive during conversations."

Now, choose your visual cue and develop a sentence to describe it.

Reflect on Your Active Listening Progress Before Sleep

Reflection is critical to growth. Before you go to bed, take a moment to reflect on your day. How well did you practice active listening? Did you encounter any challenges or successes? Write a brief note in your journal to track your progress. For instance, you can ask yourself: "Did I actively listen during my lunchtime conversation with my friend? How did it feel?"

Your reflection would look like, "Today, I actively listened during my lunchtime conversation with my friend. I focused on maintaining eye contact and nodding to show my interest. It felt great to connect and understand their perspective."

Now, write a brief note to reflect on your active listening progress.

Partnering Up for Mutual Support

Team up for success. Enlist the support of a loved one or a friend committed to active listening. Hold each other accountable by reminding and encouraging one another to stay attentive during conversations. You can check in with each other daily and share your active listening experiences. For instance, you decide to partner up with your friend Sarah and remind each other to stay present and share your active listening wins at the end of the day.

Pro Tip: Use active listening when you are communicating about active listening.

Here's an example of what your check-in could look like:

"Hey, how did it go today? How was your active listening practice?"

Now, decide how you'll partner up for mutual support.

Maintain a Listening Journal to Track Experiences and Growth

Journal your journey. Keeping a journal will help you track your active listening experiences and growth. Note down instances where you felt you actively listened, moments of challenge, and any insights you gained. Write down any instances when someone actively listened to you or when you did not feel heard. Over time, you'll observe your progress as an active listener. Use prompts like "Describe a situation where I successfully practiced active listening today" or "What challenges did I face in staying attentive during a conversation?"

For instance, you could write, "Today, I talked with my neighbor and actively listened to their gardening stories. It was challenging to stay focused, but I tried to nod and maintain eye contact. I learned more about their passion for gardening and felt more connected."

Now, create a prompt for your listening journal:

Your Final Plan for Staying an Active Listener

It's time to bring it all together and create your plan for staying an active listener. Use the strategies above as a starting point, and customize them to fit your lifestyle and preferences. Write down your plan in your journal or notebook. Remember that consistency and intention are vital to making active listening a natural part of your interactions.

1. Set a daily intention for active listening:
    - Example: During our evening together, I make a point to actively listen to my partner as she talks about her day.
2. Use my visual cue to refocus:
    - Example: I will keep a small pebble on my desk and touch it during conversations.
3. Reflect on my active listening progress before sleep:
    - Example: Did I actively listen during my team meeting? How can I improve tomorrow?
4. Partner up with:
    - Example: I'll partner with my sibling, and we will text each other about our active listening efforts.
5. Maintain my listening journal:
    - Example: Describe a situation where I encountered challenges in active listening and how I overcame them.

By implementing these practical reminders and customizing them to your unique circumstances, you'll be well on your way to making active listening a habitual and enriching part of your daily life.

Congratulations to You

Congratulations on your commitment to becoming a skilled and empathetic active listener! In the next and final chapter, you will find information on some other inspirational writers and information on some of the sources that were used to write this book. Check them out if you want to dive even deeper into the beautiful world of listening! If you don´t, that is okay. By reading this book and doing the exercises, you have already gained a solid foundation for practicing active listening skills and taking your relationship to new heights!

I know that there are plenty of great books about communication out there, and I'm so grateful that you choose to read this book all the way to the end! I hope you found it really helpful, and if you did, please tell me so in the reviews. On the other hand, if you find it boring or unhelpful, please let me know! Your thoughts and input are really valuable to me – I promise to read and consider every word.

With Love

Suzanne C Carlsson

Inspiration and References

As you continue your exploration of active listening beyond these pages, drawing inspiration from renowned experts and resources is valuable. Here are some influential figures and resources that can further enrich your understanding and practice of active listening:

Carl Rogers

Carl Rogers, a distinguished psychologist and one of the founders of humanistic psychology has made significant contributions to the study of active listening. His work, particularly in the book "On Becoming a Person," underscores the importance of empathic listening in establishing meaningful connections and promoting personal growth. Rogers' insights into creating a safe and non-judgmental space for open dialogue can deeply inform your active listening journey.

Central to Rogers' philosophy is the notion of "unconditional positive regard." This concept encapsulates accepting and valuing individuals without judgment or conditions. In active listening, practicing unconditional positive regard entails suspending preconceived notions and embracing a noncritical stance. This genuine acceptance paves the way for authentic conversations where both parties feel valued and understood.

Rogers' pioneering work extended beyond theoretical concepts and found its application in therapy. He introduced client-centered treatment, emphasizing the therapist's empathic understanding, genuineness, and unconditional positive regard. This therapeutic approach not only revolutionized the field of psychology but also underscored the significance of active listening in creating a healing and transformative environment.

Graham D. Bodie

Graham D. Bodie's scholarly pursuits led him to examine the art and science of listening with a keen and discerning eye. His research spans various contexts, from interpersonal relationships to healthcare settings, workplace dynamics, and beyond. Through his meticulous studies, Bodie has offered valuable insights into how active listening influences communication outcomes and shapes the quality of connections.

One of Bodie's notable contributions is his exploration of active listening within healthcare. His research delves into the interactions between patients and medical professionals, highlighting how attentive and empathic listening can enhance patient satisfaction, improve treatment adherence, and contribute to better health outcomes. By uncovering the profound implications of active listening in healthcare settings, Bodie underscores its potential to humanize and optimize medical care.

In the ever-evolving landscape of professional interactions, Bodie's research illuminates the impact of active listening on workplace dynamics. His studies reveal how practical listening skills enhance team collaboration, leadership effectiveness, and employee engagement. By recognizing the pivotal role of active listening in achieving workplace harmony and productivity, Bodie's work offers valuable insights for individuals and organizations alike.

John M. Gottman

In relationship science, few names resonate as strongly as John M. Gottman, a pioneering psychologist, and researcher renowned for his extensive investigations into the dynamics of human connections. With a focus on couples and relationships, Gottman's groundbreaking work delves into the intricate dance of communication, and his insights underscore the pivotal role of active listening in fostering lasting and harmonious bonds.

John M. Gottman's research has been instrumental in unraveling the language of love and understanding within intimate partnerships. Through rigorous studies and comprehensive observations, Gottman illuminated how active listening is a cornerstone of successful relationships. His pioneering research methods, often involving in-depth analysis of real-life interactions, have provided valuable insights into the nuances of effective communication and empathic understanding.

One of Gottman's most notable contributions is developing the "Sound Relationship House" theory, which encompasses the essential components of a thriving partnership. At the heart of this construct lies attunement: being tuned in and actively listening to one another's thoughts, feelings, and experiences. Gottman's research underscores that fostering a secure emotional connection requires cultivating empathy and practicing genuine active listening.

International Listening Association (ILA)

In the landscape of effective communication, the International Listening Association (ILA) stands as a beacon of knowledge, research, and advocacy. It is dedicated to often overlooked yet profoundly impactful listening skills. Founded on the principle that listening is a cornerstone of meaningful human interaction, ILA has championed this essential art's study, practice, and teaching, shedding light on the transformative power of active listening.

ILA is a global hub that brings together scholars, practitioners, educators, and enthusiasts united by their shared passion for understanding and promoting effective listening. By fostering a vibrant community of individuals committed to advancing listening skills, ILA has created a platform for collaboration and the exchange of best practices.

At the heart of ILA's mission lies a dedication to advancing the field of listening through rigorous research and scholarly exploration. The organization provides a conduit for researchers to publish their findings, contributing to a growing body of knowledge that underscores the multifaceted benefits of active listening. Through conferences, journals, and publications, ILA facilitates the dissemination of cutting-edge insights illuminating the intricate nuances of attentive understanding.

Brene Brown

Brene Brown, a renowned researcher and storyteller, emphasizes the power of vulnerability and empathy in building genuine connections. Her work highlights how active listening aligns with compassion and wholehearted living principles. Exploring Brown's writings and talks provides valuable insights into how active listening creates a more empathetic and understanding world.

Brene Brown's groundbreaking research on vulnerability has challenged societal norms and encouraged a radical shift in how you perceive and engage with your imperfections. Through her famous TED Talk on "The Power of Vulnerability" and subsequent publications, including books like "Daring Greatly" and "Rising Strong," Brown invites us to recognize vulnerability as a catalyst for meaningful human connection. By embracing and sharing your vulnerabilities with others, you create a space for open dialogue and mutual understanding.

Dale Carnegie

Dale Carnegie's legacy is perhaps best encapsulated in his famous book "How to Win Friends and Influence People." This literary gem, published in 1936, remains a cornerstone in the self-help genre and a testament to Carnegie's profound understanding of human behavior. His principles emphasize the importance of genuine connection, active listening, and meaningful communication as pathways to success in both personal and professional spheres.

Carnegie's teachings encourage continuous self-improvement and personal growth. He champions the idea that through effective communication and empathetic listening, you can positively influence your interactions and inspire change in others. It aligns seamlessly with the transformative potential of active listening, which empowers us to contribute positively to the lives of those around us.

Marshall B. Rosenberg

Marshall Rosenberg's Nonviolent Communication (NVC) has significantly enriched the practice of active listening. NVC emphasizes empathetic and compassionate communication, fostering more profound understanding and connection between individuals. It encourages active listeners to go beyond surface-level comprehension and truly engage with others' feelings and needs.

Incorporating NVC principles into active listening involves hearing words and deciphering the underlying emotions and motivations. By focusing on observations, feelings, needs, and requests, active listeners using NVC create a safe space for open dialogue. This approach facilitates constructive conversations, reduces conflicts, and nurtures empathy – all integral components of effective active listening that contribute to more meaningful and harmonious relationships.

Conclusion

These references and inspirations begin your ongoing journey as an active listener. By immersing yourself in the insights of these experts and exploring their works, you can deepen your understanding of active listening's profound impact on relationships, communication, and personal growth. As you navigate the dynamic landscape of human interaction, remember that your commitment to active listening transforms your conversations and connection with the world around you.

As you continue your practice of active listening, remember that the journey is continuous and ever-evolving. The skills you've cultivated throughout this workbook will be a solid foundation for a lifetime of meaningful and enriching connections. Thank you for embarking on this transformative journey. May your commitment to active listening lead you to a world of deeper understanding, empathy, and genuine human connection.

References

(c) Copyright skillsyouneed.com 2011-. (n.d.). Active listening. Skillsyouneed.com. https://www.skillsyouneed.com/ips/active-listening.html

(N.d.). Indeed.com. https://in.indeed.com/career-advice/career-development/active-listening-skills

Arlin Cuncic, M. A. (2010, May 10). Seven active listening techniques to practice in your daily conversations. Verywell Mind. https://www.verywellmind.com/what-is-active-listening-3024343

British Heart Foundation. (2023, December 6). Active listening. British Heart Foundation. https://www.bhf.org.uk/informationsupport/heart-matters-magazine/wellbeing/how-to-talk-about-health-problems/active-listening

Doyle, A. (2015, January 2). Active listening definition, skills, and examples. The Balance. https://www.thebalancemoney.com/active-listening-skills-with-examples-2059684

Expert Panel®. (2023, February 3). Fifteen key tips for developing active listening skills as A leader. Forbes. https://www.forbes.com/sites/forbesbusinesscouncil/2023/02/03/15-key-tips-for-developing-active-listening-skills-as-a-leader/

How to use active listening skills to coach others. (2023, February 2). CCL; Center for Creative Leadership. https://www.ccl.org/articles/leading-effectively-articles/coaching-others-use-active-listening-skills/

MindTools. (n.d.-a). Mindtools.com. https://www.mindtools.com/ai4ff5e/how-good-are-your-listening-skills

MindTools. (n.d.-b). Mindtools.com. https://www.mindtools.com/az4wxv7/active-listening

What is active listening? (2021). https://doi.org/10.4135/9781529763164

www.ingramcontent.com/pod-product-compliance
Lightning Source LLC
LaVergne TN
LVHW010657200726
843507LV00011B/1916